Becoming What I Am

Becoming What I Am

A discussion of the methods and results of Christian prayer

H. A. WILLIAMS CR

Darton, Longman and Todd
London

First published in Great Britain in 1977 by
Darton, Longman and Todd Ltd
89 Lillie Road, London SW6 1UD

5th printing 1985

This edition 1991

British Library Cataloguing in Publication Data
Williams, H. A. (Harry Abbott)
  Becoming what I am : discussion of the methods and
  results of Christian prayer.
  1. Christianity. Prayer
  I. Title
  248.32

ISBN 0–232–51952–8

Printed and bound in Great Britain by
Courier International Ltd, Tiptree, Essex

To John Betjeman

(because he likes dim things)
with love and admiration

Contents

Contents

Preface

There is nothing in these talks which has not been said before by others. The requests for their publication must be due to the atmosphere of St Mary's, Bourne Street, where they were delivered. I am grateful to the Vicar, John Gilling, for the kindness of his hospitality.

I have said nothing about the great political, economic, and sociological problems which confront our society. Obviously they are of central importance to christian concern. But I am sure that matters of such enormous complexity demand to be considered by christians who are both informed about and experienced in public affairs to a depth and degree to which I cannot begin to attain.

Yet a fundamental spiritual dimension of all social problems is the fact of human solidarity, that all men everywhere are most deeply interconnected, that everybody is my neighbour and my neighbour is myself. And this truth I have tried to explore a little in what I have said about prayer as intercession.

God's love for me is His love for the world. And so too will be my love for Him, if it is genuine. It will manifest itself in an outgoingness to others, though

11

there is no standard ready-made form in which that outgoingness must necessarily be clothed – a fact which zealous christian social reformers or revolutionaries are sometimes tempted to forget.

In any case, for all its essential communal context, God's love must first be apprehended as His love for me. Otherwise it is not apprehended as love, but only as benevolence or goodwill which fail to satisfy because they fall infinitely short of what love is. It is only to the degree in which I begin to apprehend God's love for me that I can begin to apprehend His love for all men. And that is the mainspring of all christian social action.

Prayer begins as the opening of my heart and mind to God's love for me. And it never ceases to be that however wide, and indeed universal, the implications and demands of that love are discovered to be. When, on the other hand, christian public political action begins to be divorced from the tender intimate love which gave it birth, it begins to become a power-game and as such no less a denial of God's love than the evil it opposes. Causes begin to matter more than people and the Son of God is on the way to being crucified afresh in the name of righteousness and by campaigns and committees. For how can I love my neighbour as myself unless I am deeply aware of what I am, that I am being loved into fullness of life by the Father of us all?

H.A.W.

1. Introduction

The talks on which this book is based were advertised as a 'school of prayer', and the word school may conjure up visions of a schoolmaster. But I can't be that. Indeed, it is only as a matter of convention that I was advertised as giving talks on prayer at all, because a speaker is at least supposed to be more informed than his audience, to be some sort of expert on the subject about which he speaks. But I have no claim whatever to be an expert on prayer, which I often find extremely difficult, sometimes very boring, and always rather baffling. And it can at times leave me feeling frustrated because I appear to have done nothing and nothing appears to have happened so that by the end I am almost downright angry. I read a number of those wonderful books about the spiritual life which, while I am reading them, appear to offer me a recipe which will turn me on. But when I then later try to put theory into practice, I generally find that after all I am back again at square one. And perhaps the only sign of divine grace of which I am aware is that instead of feeling angry, sometimes I want to laugh; to laugh at the apparent absurdity of the whole enterprise of prayer. And that laughter, I have come to think, is indeed what I have just called it, a sign of grace, a sign of God's coming to me. It is, if you like, an angel of the Lord. For we laugh at what is funny, and the essence of funny things is their incongruity. When you really think that something is a real horse and then discover that it is only a pantomime horse, that is what is funny. Or, when Charlie Chaplin pats and caresses the small child who has repeatedly kicked him so long as the child's parents are in the room, but kicks the child back as soon as the parents have gone, that is what is funny. So, the angel of laughter is the revelation of the incongruous. And when the angel comes to us as we are trying to pray, what is revealed to us is the incongruity of our attempts at prayer.

The incongruity consists of our making into a matter of vast complication what is in fact something we can't do because it is so simple.

It is simple for us to walk from here to Sloane Square. But imagine some eccentric who made it into an abstruce mathematical operation involving geometry, logarithms and heaven knows what. I hope we should laugh at him, because that man is often us when we pray. To commune with God in prayer we haven't even got to walk a hundred yards because God is always with us, nearer to us than the air we breathe, and He is always waiting upon us everywhere and eagerly listening to the slightest murmur of our heart. Didn't Jesus tell us repeatedly

16

that we are the sons of our Father who is in heaven and didn't He say that unless we become as little children we can't hope to enter the Kingdom of God? Now imagine a really good home with marvellously loving parents. Wouldn't the children go to the parents naturally and simply without tying themselves into knots by working out elaborate schemes of approach and encounter? And God, remember, has no need to study Doctor Spock or even to disagree with him. So if, as I have told you I do, I find prayer difficult and baffling, that is due to my being unable when I pray to unravel myself from my own sophistication.

That sophistication is due chiefly to the fact that like almost all other people I had good parents but not perfect parents. And because my parents were not perfect parents, my approach to them as a small child was not entirely spontaneous and natural. To some extent I did have to work out schemes of approach and so on. And the attitude of the small child to less than perfect parents still persists in me now in my attitude to God. That is part of the unconscious background of my prayer. Perhaps for instance, without really knowing it, my parents demanded of me as a small child a degree of affection or achievement as a condition of acceptance. And so now I think that it is not enough simply to walk a short distance but that I have somehow to earn my passage by artificially turning that short walk into an obstacle race, a puzzle or a problem;

17

though not so much of course into an intelligence test as into a soul test, devising schemes whereby I can make the grade spiritually. But in fact there is no grade. There is only your Heavenly Father who is always more ready to hear than you to pray. And you wouldn't want to pray, you wouldn't be in the slightest degree interested, you wouldn't be here now, unless He were already within your heart and mind giving you the desire to seek and find Him. Indeed, as Pascal said, you wouldn't be seeking Him unless you had already found Him.

I have said that in this matter of prayer I am just as tied up in knots as anybody else so that I can't begin to speak as a master speaks to disciples. I can only share with you my own very limited experience of praying and my own very fallible estimates of where I have gone wrong and what I believe has been right. What therefore I have to offer you here is not instruction, but various things which have either happened to me or haven't happened. I do speak, I hope, within the community of faith, and that community of faith has provided me with the necessary context in which to discern and evaluate my experience. Indeed, that community of faith has been to me, as it must be to us all, at least in a secondary sense, my father and mother. But what parents teach us, we learn truly only by appropriating it as our very own. I am not church teaching, I am *me*, and you are not church teaching. You are *you*. I hope that within the context of the community of faith my own extremely limited experience of prayer, my mistakes and misjudgements as well as any insights which may be valid, will evoke you by agreement or disagreement to discover what is already at work in your heart and soul. Saint Paul describes the christians of Thessalonica as 'taught by God', and as far as prayer is concerned there is no other teacher. Perhaps that is what Jesus meant when he said 'Call no man father on earth'.

It is worth emphasising again – you will need to be simple in your approach to God, as simple as small children in their approach to perfect parents because our heavenly Father is always everywhere with us, and He is perfect. Over against this need for simplicity there is our sophistication, originating in our approach to less than perfect parents. We all still have a small child within us. But it is often a prematurely aged child, worldly beyond its years. And hence I think that our sophistication is in the last resort a prematurely aged (or what we like to call an adult) defensive measure. It is a protection against absolute love because we are somewhere very frightened of love without recognising at all clearly that we are. For absolute love, God's love, makes us fully ourselves, instead of the half people we generally are. And to become fully yourself is a terrible risk. It would commit you to God knows what and lead you God knows where. If I open my heart in simplicity to God's love I might soon find myself in Bangladesh or something of that sort, or I might find myself disagreeing or even agreeing with Mrs Whitehouse. Or letting in God's love might prompt me to join the Campaign for Homosexual Equality, or the Tory Party, or it might lead me actively to support the Tribune Group; it might make me concerned about the oppressed peoples of the Third World or even about my neighbour next door who is lonely. And God's love has been known to make the most respectable people enjoy a pub crawl. And letting in God's love is no guarantee at all that I will necessarily remain an enthusiastic member of the Church of England or even of the Anglo-Catholic set-up. And so, not so much in our minds consciously as in our bones unconsciously, we see to it that when we pray we keep ourselves tied up in knots. It is much safer. Let us keep on the armour of our sophistication and plump for security.

But then of course we miss the glorious liberty of the children of God. We remain half dead, too afraid to know what life is. And missing out on the splendour and warm intimacy of God's love, we become hooked on some compensatory activity like overwork or keeping up with the Jones's, or drink, or sex, or it might even be religiosity and church going. Such compensatory activities don't in practice compensate at all.

'Most probably', said G. K. Chesterton, 'we are still in Eden. It is only our eyes which have changed'. And our eyes have changed because part of us at least doesn't want to see. And so we complicate our response to our Father's love with schemes, techniques, esoteric information, charts, degrees of progress, and so on. There is a story at Mirfield* about a novice who did not stay long and had left before I arrived. This young man burst into the kitchen one morning, I was told, and said to the kitchen steward in a rapturous voice that he had reached what the charts describe as the final state of prayer, in technical language called the unitive way, announcing it as if he had climbed Everest and deserved a decoration. No wonder he left soon afterwards.

Personally, I distrust books about prayer. Their name is legion and most of them deserve a Gadarene destiny; though, of course, by no means all, and certainly not Alan Ecclestone's *Yes To God,*† which is one of the best books on prayer I have ever read.

I have come to the conclusion that when all is said and done, the only real prayer I can say is that of the blind beggar in the gospels 'Lord Jesus, that I may receive my sight'. Let me see the real root cause of that spiritual sophistication which separates me from God. Let me see God's real presence encompassing me, enfolding me, always everywhere. Let me see that wherever I am or

---

* The Community of which the author is a member.
† Darton, Longman and Todd, 1974

whatever I am doing, whether I feel tired or excited, angry or amused, a success or a failure, fed up or enthusiastic, a bundle of nerves or calm and quiet, miserable or happy, optimistic or in despair, whatever it may be, let me see that all I have to do is to turn simply to God and say 'Hello, it is me'. There is no need to stand on ceremony because I am at home in my Father's house. And there is no need to keep up appearances by pretending that I am a worse person than I am, or even a better person, because God knows what I am like infinitely better than I do myself. 'Hello, it is me, Your old friend and Your old enemy, Your loving friend who often neglects You, Your complicated friend, Your utterly perplexed and decidedly resentful friend, partly loving, partly hating, partly not caring. It is me'. When in your heart you even half say that (which means you half don't say it) maybe in a queue waiting for a bus which doesn't come, then there is joy in heaven among the angels of God.

'Hello, it is me', that is an answer to a prayer as well as a prayer itself because it means that we have already somehow said 'Lord Jesus, that I may receive my sight', and our sight has been given us to recognise God's presence with us, His love, and to accept it simply like a child accepting a present. But like a wise parent God will not give us everything at once because everything at once would not simply be bad for us but would literally destroy us, driving us insane. So in giving us our sight, God will probably clap upon our eyes a pair of very dark sunglasses. We must remember that when God looks a bit grey or even so depressingly grey that He is hardly visible. It doesn't mean that He isn't there or that we are blind. It means that we are in danger of seeing too much, of seeing more than we can stand. 'Hello, it is me, in those very dark glasses You fixed on my eyes. Can't You change them for glasses a little less dark?' And God *will* of course when our eyes are up to it. And He will make them up to it as the time goes on. After all God made the eyes of our soul in the first place, or rather He is making them now.

Let us put this in another way, using a different image or parable which, although it has to do with the sun, won't fit into the parable of the sunglasses (Parables don't fit into each other. It is no good asking what the good shepherd was doing when the prodigal son was in the far country.) Some of you on holiday will have had experience of a hot sunny climate when it is dark and cloudy. Let us say you are in Marrakesch and a sirocco has blown up filling the air with Sahara sand so that the sky looks dull and dark. You may imagine that you have no need to protect yourself against the sun in the usual way. At the end of the day you will have learnt your mistake. The sun was indeed there in spite of all appearances to the contrary and it will have burnt you badly. The point I want to make here is not the burning but the real presence of the sun in spite of the dark sky. So God is really present when He doesn't seem to be.

But we must not end with a parable because that might put off the clever people. So instead let us end with a grandiloquent phrase: God is now creating our spiritual vision. He is leading us to simplicity.

2. Practical Preparation

I remember when some eighteen or twenty years ago Her Majesty the Queen paid an official visit to my college at Cambridge, how marvellously she was dressed; her costume (it was a shade of green) was absolutely simple. It looked the natural and entirely unostentatious expression of herself. At a subsequent luncheon in the college dining hall, I said something to the wife of a colleague about the simplicity of the Queen's clothes. 'Yes', the wife answered, 'she really does look marvellous. But that complete simplicity, you know, is the result of the highest possible skill on the part of her couturier'.

That incident serves very well to sum up the paradox of simplicity. Far from being an easy option, simplicity from one point of view is an extremely difficult thing to achieve. It is the result of maturity, one of the fruits of discipline and experience. God leads us in our prayers to simplicity. We need to be led there because we are by no means there already. Perhaps we could put it this way: by nature we are complicated, because by nature we are fallen. It is only by grace that we can become simple. That it is only by grace that we can

27

become simple is a fact which should inspire us with the greatest possible hope. Hopes can let us down when they are centred on human persons because human persons change or can be the victims of misfortune. But God doesn't change, nor can His loving will be finally thwarted. And His will for us is that we should love and trust Him in simplicity. In other words, if it is only by grace that we can become simple, there is no room left for doubt or fear, since God always gives us His grace freely. We don't have to earn it or make the grade. It is a free gift which God gives us because He is like that. 'Before they call I will answer, while they are yet speaking I will hear'. So the labourers in the vineyard get their money only because it is the owner's good will to give it to them. The amount of work done is just not considered at the pay desk.

There is, however, one fundamental mistake which I think we must avoid. God's grace, as I have said, is freely given to us, but it works by means of what we are and not in spite of what we are. God knows I am not a heresy hunter. Indeed in the matter of heresy I am more often the fox than the hounds, and I am terrified by the ecclesiastics' equivalent of tally-ho. None the less, I can often see why certain ideas and doctrines were rejected by the ancient church as untrue because they seem to be equally untrue when they are worked out in our own lives. One heresy condemned in the early days was the notion that in Jesus Christ the divine nature completely swallowed up the human nature, so that none of the human nature was left. In Jesus you had God only, not man. To reject that view, as the church rejected it decisively, is to understand how God's grace freely given must work by means of what we are and can't work in spite of what we are. The most damnable form of spiritual pride is the attempt to live like a monophysite Christ (that is a Christ with only one nature, the divine), trying to persuade ourselves that all we need is angels' food, when in fact what we really need may well be a pint at the local. (I suppose though that the Publican must beware of thanking God that he is not like this Pharisee – which needs saying because the real Pharisee nowadays seems often to be dressed in Publican's clothing.) Anyhow, God is leading us towards simplicity, to childlike trust in Him and love for Him by his freely given grace which is His own divine presence at work within us. And His grace works not in spite of what we are but by means of what we are. In other words, we draw near to simplicity to the degree in which we become our full true selves.

But what then is my full true self? Saint Paul gave us the answer when he said it was the measure of the stature of the fullness of Christ. But, Saint Paul tells us, Christ's identity is a corporate one needing for its fullness the combination of many distinct members. Hence to grow into Christ is not to smother or swamp our individuality. On the contrary it is to affirm and ensure it. The more God's presence works within me, the more of His grace I receive, the more I shall become that unique individual person called Harry Williams. And when in some unforseeable and unimaginable future beyond this world I shall have reached the measure of the stature of the fullness of Christ, when Christ will have been perfectly formed in me, I shall still be Harry Williams.

Before, however, we get too intoxicated by visions of our ultimate future, perhaps we ought to return to the sober realities of the present. Unique as a person I may be, but another fact about me is that I am undisguisedly middle class. Most of us are middle class nowadays. That is what education has done for us. And therefore if God's grace works by means of what we are, then it follows that in us His grace will work by means of our middle classness. And that I imagine is for us our first lesson in the art of simplicity. In case you find that depressing, let me remind you that at least in the past hundred years the middle classes have produced by far the most effective and creative rebels and reformers. Both Karl Marx and Lenin came from impeccably middle-class backgrounds.

Of course I am not blowing a class trumpet nor am I doing the opposite, using the term middle class in a derogatory sense like the late Lord Robert Cecil, who used to refer to most people as an MCM, a middle-class monster. Nor am I advocating fascism or communism or even the Liberal Party. I am referring to the fact that we are educated folk, that we are capable of reading, that we can find out where our nearest Public Library is and how to use it, and that we are capable to some extent at least of organising our time. So that even though we are all of us very busy and preoccupied with a thousand things to do, we can nonetheless set regular periods apart (half an hour a week, say) for reading. I hope you don't think that monks* live in splendid idleness, gloriously ignorant of what work and chores mean, so that they can spend twenty-four hours a day contemplating the heavenly host. Laying supper or washing up for seventy or eighty people is sometimes the least of what they have to do.

I am boasting but then Saint Paul boasted, and I don't really see why I should have to pretend to be holier than he was. But the point I am making is that because God works by means of what we are, that for us means that he works within us by means of our ability to read. He leads us to the simplicity of our full selves by our ability to feed our minds by books. I am not referring to the devotional use of books, whatever that means, but to reading in the ordinary sense. What we are to read will depend upon our particular temperaments, interests and circumstances, and we shall certainly need advice about it. It is necessary to emphasise the immense

* The author is a member of the Anglican Community of the Resurrection.

importance of reading, since the average educated
English lay Christian seems to me too often
horrifyingly ignorant about Christian doctrine,
Christian history, the relation of Christianity to
other world faiths, how Christianity fits into a com-
prehensive view of life and the universe, how contemporary scholarship has opened up our understanding of the Bible, and the relation of faith to
morals, of what we believe to what we do. There are
good books for the general reader on all these topics
available at our public libraries. We shall, of course,
be able to follow up only one department of enquiry
among those I have described. And in addition to
these books for the average reader, many of us will
need to read the works of great writers, poets and
novelists, as well as theologians and philosophers.
By reading in this quite ordinary sense we shall ex-
ercise our intelligence and stir up our imagination.
And because we are educated people, this enrich-
ment of our mind and hence of our imagination is a
very important preliminary to prayer. It may oc-
casionally work directly, so that what we have read
will form part of the content of our thoughts and
feelings as we lift up our hearts to God. But in my
experience reading books doesn't often work directly like that. Generally, what we have read will have
been for the most part forgotten, and even that part
which is remembered won't generally bear any
direct impact upon our prayers. I think St.
Augustine can help us here. St. Augustine uses the

word memory, *memoria,* to describe not what we remember in the ordinary sense, but all the experiences, impressions and ideas which have impinged upon us and which are now stored somewhere within us even though in the ordinary sense we have forgotten most of them. By memory St. Augustine meant something very like what today we call the unconscious. And the most important part of us which is fed by what we read is our unconscious minds. Ideas impinge upon us as we read and we then apparently forget them, or most of them. But we don't therefore lose them. They remain with us in what St. Augustine called our memory. They thus help to make us what we are, and to repeat it again, it is by means of what we are that God works within us.

For various reasons our prayer may remain cold and dry even though we are regular readers. But if we don't ever read books about our Christian faith then our failure to do so may well be an important contributory cause of our prayer being dead and unreal. The leaven hasn't the dough to work on. Grace has been denied the nature it needs to inhabit and transform. God's Word can't become incarnate within us because we haven't given it the flesh to do so. We are trying to have God by escaping from what we are instead of by growing into what we are.

To use a completely different image: household coal. Coal is heavy and sometimes damp. It requires quite a lot of energy to carry it about and in itself it gives no warmth at all. Who would like to spend a freezing night locked in a coal cellar? Of course the parallel is far from perfect, since reading can often be a stimulating experience. But as far as our prayers are concerned, what we read is often like the coal we keep in the cellar. It doesn't of itself generate spiritual warmth, and it may remain for a long period in the cellar of our mind or what St. Augustine called our memory. But the time will come when the coal will be used, or at least some sack or other of it. That is to say the time will come when the fire of God's presence within us will play upon the mental coal we have accumulated, and then the coal will contribute mightily to the warmth and reality of our prayer. And when that happens, it is worth pointing out, we shall almost certainly not be aware of what particular sack of coal it is on which the fire of God's love is playing. And we shan't want to know. We shall be enjoying the fire, not thinking about the coal. But the coal will still be a necessary part of the fire. We have to trust God to use our mental coal as and when He sees fit, for it is His business to know when the time is ripe. He may keep us waiting for quite a long time. He kept some of the saints waiting for years. Our part of the business is to see that the cellar of our mind and memory is kept reasonably well stocked. That is all we can do. But it is both essential and enough.

How odd it is from one point of view to long for

eternity and to be sent to the Public Library. If we weren't so middle class we might find God in a stable. But stables don't feature much, if at all, in our lives except as folksy things, and God is never found in the folksy. He is found only in the commonplace. For that is what the original stable in Bethlehem was, commonplace. Acceptance of the commonplace as the vehicle, the sacrament, of the eternal is at the very heart of Christianity. We must remember that as we set about to feed our minds. And when we have accepted the fact that for people like us the public library is one of the gates of heaven, we shall then have had a first tentative glimpse of what simplicity is.

3. Prayer as Meditation and Contemplation

In the previous two chapters I have been talking of the need for simplicity in prayer. Simplicity, we shall probably think, means being spontaneous. And there is an important sense in which prayer, if it is to be a true prayer, must be spontaneous. But we can misunderstand what spontaneity means. To be spontaneous, I take it, means to be natural, to be yourself without artifice or pretence, to say and do things which express authentically what you are. But if that is what being spontaneous means, we must notice that far from ruling out formality, spontaneity positively requires it. Take social life, for instance. There would be precious little spontaneity in social life unless there were a certain degree of formality. Last time I visited this Church a lady kindly invited the Vicar and myself out to lunch. It was far from being a formal occasion. It was just a small family gathering. But formality was not absent. Our hostess went through the recognised forms of making us feel welcome and we went through the recognised forms of being grateful guests, and neither party was being in the slightest degree insincere. And because these recognised

forms existed and we used them there was
generated a genuine spontaneity. We loosened up
and were able to be our natural selves. Had there
been no recognised forms of hospitality given and
received all of us would have been thinking all the
time what to do or say next, and the last thing we
should have been is spontaneous. An example on a
deeper level is the work of any artist in whatever
medium. The artist if he is to be a true one must of
course be spontaneous, that is to say, he must give
to what is in him the most authentic expression of
which he is capable. But to do this, he must submit
to some form or other because his medium requires
it. A painter is not a painter when he strums a
piano, nor is a musician a musician when he daubs
a canvas. And the form to which the artist submits,
far from hindering his spontaneity, not only makes
it possible but evokes it. Think how the sixteenth
century form of the play or the nineteenth century
form of the novel evoked from Shakespeare and
Dickens some of the most gloriously spontaneous
writing in the English language. So if, as it does,
simplicity in prayer means being spontaneous, our
being spontaneous doesn't rule out a certain degree
of formality. On the contrary, it requires it.

There is, first of all, the formality of the time
table. It is extremely unlikely that we shall pray unless we set aside definite times to do it. And what
matters is not their length, nor their frequency but
their regularity: twice a week for ten minutes, say,

or once a week for quarter of an hour. It is better here to be under-ambitious than over-ambitious. Perhaps a way of putting this would be to say that a more exacting rule of prayer has to be earned by keeping a less exacting one. If we keep our under-ambitious rule, say for six months, then perhaps we can add to it a little. Setting aside regular times for prayer doesn't of course mean that we are not always in communion with God, or that He may not make us aware of it at any time or place, at the cinema, at the pub, waiting for a bus, going to collect the children, walking down Piccadilly, spending a day in the country, whatever it may be. Awareness of our continuous communion with God, or, more accurately, of God's continuous communion with us, may come anywhere at any time, sometimes flooding in like the sea. But because in His love God sometimes makes us wonderfully aware of His presence without our inviting Him, that is no reason for us to deny Him the courtesy of being at home to Him on regular occasions and opening the door.

As well as the formality of the timetable there is the formality of the procedure we adopt when we pray. In this connexion we must never forget that the formality of procedure is to enable us to be spontaneous. It is never formality for its own sake. If after a reasonable try-out a particular form of prayer kills off rather than enables our spontaneity, then we should drop that form for another one. In any case, most of us need to change the forms of our prayer from time to time, because a form of prayer which once was meaningful and made us aware of God's presence with us may after a time cease to do so. Maybe we shall have got out of one form of prayer all that it can give us and we need therefore to move on to another. After all, a boy of six converses with his father in a different manner from a young man of twenty. But that comparison, good in one way, is far from perfect since changing the forms of prayer isn't a matter of growing up or making progress. It is simply matching the form of prayer to the contemporary needs of our temperament and circumstances. And these change without our necessarily being more advanced or less.

Printed prayers like the Lord's Prayer, the *Anima Christi*, or one of the collects in the Prayer Book, when said slowly and thoughtfully, is one form of prayer. And such prayers are for many people the formal vehicle by means of which in heart and mind they ascend to God. Sometimes they need to change the particular printed prayers they use for others and there are of course books of such prayers available. We must not be spiritually snobbish about printed prayers, as if using them were a second or third rate form of devotion. If we find that they enable us to realise God's presence with us and to hold converse with Him, then nothing could be better. But many people find that after a time printed prayers become meaningless, no more than a jumble of words and that therefore far from enabling their prayer, it strangles it. And that is a sign that they need to move on to another form of prayer.

A form of prayer like everything else worth doing demands some simple commonsense preparation. If we need to move from printed prayers to something else we must decide what the something else is and then have it ready in some manageably practical form. The new form of our prayer will probably consist not this time of reading through a printed prayer thoughtfully, but of thinking over certain ideas in a certain sequence. It may be a story from the gospels; or a passage from the Old Testament, or a book outside the Bible by somebody who has been seeking God. The simple commonsense preparation here consists of having the passages we are going to think over ready and divided up for our use. It is no good deciding that we are going to think over the Bible, or the Gospels, or St. Paul's Epistles or the writing of Teilhard de Chardin unless we first take the trouble to select pieces of suitable length and content for the purpose we have in mind.

For the sake of example, let us say that I have decided to think over the parables in St. Matthew's gospel, making a note of chapter and verse of the parables and selecting a parable for each of the days of the week on which I have decided to practise this form of prayer.

Then I decide what time of day and in what place I shall be most free from interference. Suppose I have decided to spend ten minutes twice a week during the lunch hour in the church down the street. I have already divided the book I am going to use into suitable sections, so I go into the church, I am still for a moment to remember God's real and enclosing presence with me. I tell Him that I am putting myself at His disposal for the next ten minutes and that I trust Him to teach me what He knows I need to learn, even if it be only patience, the ability to wait without fretting. I then sit down and read through the passage I have chosen, think it over carefully and see whether it has any particular application to my life at the moment. Sometimes, a message will seem to get through to me from God, either about Himself and His love or about what He requires of me – to trust Him more, for instance. The ten minutes will sometimes pass in a flash. It will sometimes seem like five hours and sometimes like ten minutes. But none of that matters one way or the other. What matters is that you trust God enough to put yourself at His disposal by practising this form of prayer for ten minutes twice a week. What happens is up to God, not you. Thank him if and when He makes you warmly and gloriously aware of the splendour of His love. Thank Him too if He doesn't; because it is easy enough to fall into a kind of spiritual cupboard-love, loving God chiefly and only for the delightful feelings we have when we pray. When we appear to be sent away empty, we are in fact filled with good things, not only discovering the happiness of patience but also taking the first small step towards true love: the love which is the reflection or echo of God's own giving love. So, when you settle down for your ten minutes and nothing happens and it seems like five hours, God is giving you the opportunity of being led to the love which is a giving of yourself to Him and not a getting. And that love of yours will be also His love.

We shall often be besieged by wandering and irrevelant thoughts. When that happens we must remember that we are much more than the thoughts which wander. While on the surface of our mind we are reminding ourselves that we must collect a suit from the cleaners or wondering whether Mrs. Smith enjoyed the concert last night, we may be in active communion with God on a deeper level of our mind. So when our thoughts wander it doesn't mean that all we are is wandering. I am quite sure that trying desperately to concentrate on the superficial level of the mind is a mistake. We must just recall that superficial level to where we really and profoundly are, even if we have to recall it a dozen times a minute.

But when we try this kind of prayer we can be besieged not only by wandering irrelevant thoughts but also sometimes by feelings of savage hatred against somebody or resentment; some smouldering anger, some corrosive anxiety, some deadening sense of depression. If we find ourselves in that sort of state we can say: 'Oh God, I am hellishly angry; I think so and so is a swine; I am tortured by worry about this or that; I am pretty certain that I have missed my chances in life; this or that has left me feeling terribly depressed. But nonetheless here I am like this, feeling both bloody and bloodyminded, and I am going to stay here for ten minutes and use my book. You are most unlikely to give me anything. I know that. But I am going to stay for the ten minutes nonetheless'. If you can say something like that, it shows how very near to God you in fact are in spite of your feelings. Or perhaps better, not in spite of your feelings but because of them.

But how can you be close to God because you are feeling angry or resentful or worried or depressed? Well, the New Testament often speaks of Christ's sufferings, His passion, death and resurrection as a conflict and a victory. Christ in His passion is in conflict with all the destructive forces in the world, and by His passion he overcomes destructiveness and wins the day for creativeness. That is what His resurrection shows forth, the victory of creative love over everything that destroys. Christ sometimes invites us, especially when we pray, (though not only when we pray) to share His conflict with Him. Our feelings of anger, worry, depression or whatever, are signs that for the time being Christ is calling us to

46

stand with Him in the thick of the battle, to face within us the forces of destruction. And since it is with Christ that we are standing in the thick of the battle, then although we will probably continue to feel bloody and bloodyminded, in deepest reality Christ's victory over destructiveness will be working itself out within us and by means of us. That is what St. Paul meant when he said that in the degree in which we share the fellowship of Christ's sufferings, to that degree we are also partakers of the power of His resurrection. So if on occasion you have not so much a boring as a bad time when you pray, with the noise of passions apparently ringing you for dead unto a place where is no rest, then remember what is really happening. It is Christ within you feeling the onslaughts of destructiveness and thereby winning the day for His own creative love. By your bad time at prayer you are being the agent of Christ restoring, saving love. And not just for yourself but for mankind. For in the invisible world we are all most deeply interconnected. No man is an island. No man can live for himself alone or die for himself alone or suffer for himself alone. What happens to us when we pray is happening for all men everywhere.

But of course, our time at prayer won't always be boring or bad. Often we shall be aware of the peace of God, of His majesty and His mercy, of His warm intimate love for us and of His glory. Sometimes it will be as if we were in a small boat gently floating down a stream. If that happens, then don't use the oars any more. In other words, don't stick to the passage of the book you have chosen. Don't go on thinking it out. The book has done its work. By means of it you have rowed yourself out into the middle of the stream, and the stream itself will now take you along. You can rest as you float on, rest in the presence of God and enjoy the stillness of eternity without any more internal chattering. You haven't got to get anywhere, because you are already there. 'Be still and know that I am God' – that will have become true of you. Sometimes you will have to row, think over the passage of the book. Sometimes you will find that you can abandon yourself straightaway to the stream.

Von Hügel once said that a very fruitful form of prayer could be compared to sucking a lozenge. What he meant was that instead of selecting passages for meditation in the way I have described, you read through a suitable book, but not in the ordinary way of getting through it. You read a few lines or a paragraph and then ponder over it. It may say something to you or make you aware of God's presence, perhaps for the whole ten minutes. Or perhaps the lines you read will keep you going for only a minute or two; then you can go on to the next few lines and try them out. On some days you will find that two lines of the book will fill up ten minutes prayer time, and on other days that you will have to read eight or nine pages. But your aim will be not to swallow what you read immediately as in ordinary reading, but to keep it in your mouth and feel its flavour, as you do a lozenge.

Our job is to put ourselves at God's disposal by the discipline of regularity, by faithfulness to our rule, and by the use of that common sense without which we can't do anything. But there our job ends. What happens when we pray is God's business, not ours. God will give us what He knows is best. And what is best we see in the life of Jesus, in His joy and peace and stillness and confidence and trust. And also in His passion, His bloody sweat, His death and resurrection.

4. Prayer as Petition

This chapter is concerned with prayer as petition, asking God for things.

There is no doubt that the New Testament teaches us to ask God for things. Jesus said 'Ask and it shall be given unto you', and St. Paul tells us to let our requests be known unto God, while the Epistle of St. James tells us bluntly: 'You do not have because you do not ask'. There is a certain kind of spiritual snobbery which thinks itself above asking God for things. And such snobbery is condemned not only by the passages I have just quoted but also by one of the most sacred moments in all history, when Jesus in the Garden of Gethsemane made *de profundis* the request: 'If it be possible let this cup pass from me'. So true prayer includes asking for things. There can be no doubt whatever about that.

At the same time we must be very careful to distinguish true prayer from its perverted parody. I am referring to magic. You sometimes hear Christians say 'I believe in magic', as though that were a statement of faith and devotion. But if it is, they are misusing the word magic. Magic means manipulating the supernatural, God, to serve your own purposes. 'My will be done, O God, and I am going to get you by prayer to do it. I want a certain horse to win the 3.30 and by my prayers I am going to make it win'. That is magic. Of course, we seldom express it to ourselves as directly or as crudely as that, but it is often there as a kind of background atmosphere. It is as though we had made a bargain with God in which we undertake something, not necessarily prayer in the literal sense but, shall we say, leading a decent life, on the understanding that God will respond by giving us good luck or at least by preserving us from bad luck. There is an amusing description of this almost unconscious religion of the average Englishman in P. G. Wodehouse's story *Big Money*. The young Lord Biskerton, commonly known as 'the biscuit', gets a red hot tip from the stockmarket which promises to bring him a shower of gold. From his earliest years, we read, "the biscuit had nourished an unwavering conviction that providence was saving up something particularly juicy in the way of rewards for him, and that it was only a matter of time before providence came across and delivered the goods. Lord Biskerton based his belief on the fact that he had always tried to be a reasonably bonhomous sort of chap and was one who like Abu Ben Adhem loved his fellow men. Abu had clicked, and Lord Biskerton expected to click. But not in his most sanguine moments had he ever expected to click on this colossal scale. It just showed that when providence knew it had got hold of a good man, the sky was the limit." As we might expect, the red hot tip doesn't pay off.

But if the prayer of petition isn't magic, manipulating God in some way or other to give us what we want, then what is it? I suggest that the prayer of petition is the courage of honesty in the presence of God, the courage before God of being what we are, everything we are without evasion.

Sometimes I shall completely approve of what I really am and think it right. And other times I shan't be too sure. Perhaps in what I want I am being just a bit selfish, perhaps not. At other times again I shall very much disapprove (or at least a part of me will) of what I really am and really want. Let us take each of these in term.

The doctors, let us say, have diagnosed that I have a kidney complaint but assert that, circumstances being favourable, it can be cured. I am a social worker doing useful work and I want to get back and resume it. Here my petition will be a prayer for complete recovery. And unless I can thus ask God to restore me to health, then God isn't what Jesus said He is: 'my Father'. My petition here will be the natural request of a child who trusts and loves. And God is inviting me to use my kidney disease as an opportunity to grow in my trust in Him and love for Him. So without hesitation I can pray 'Oh God, make me well'.

But take another case: I am not at all rich, but I have a job which is reasonably well paid, and this enables me to keep my wife and family in reasonable comfort. But my job is threatened; maybe I shall be declared redundant. However, I am luckier than most people because a friend of mine has offered me another job if my present job falls through, but this other job is not nearly so well paid. It would cut my salary by half, and the inconvenience and privation which would result are obvious. It would put an awful strain not only upon myself, but upon my family. So, with the courage of honesty in the presence of God, I pray that I may keep my present job. Perhaps I am thinking too much of myself and of my own concerns, perhaps not. Perhaps the question I am really asking myself, and it forms the background of my prayer, is: if I lose my present job, shall I be able to take the consequences of its loss without disintegrating in some way or other? And so I pray 'Oh God, let me continue in my present job. Don't let me lose it through redundancy'. That prayer is not so very different from the prayer of Jesus in Gethsemane: 'Let this cup pass from me'. It is only superficially that it sounds selfish. It is really an act of humility. I don't imagine that I am the marvellous sort of person who can take misfortune without being warped or broken. So, like Jesus, I pray for the misfortune not to happen.

But take yet another case. I am an actor with a

small part in a theatre in the West End of London. But I am also the understudy of the star. It is rumoured that the star has cancer and will not be able to go on much longer. If he leaves I shall get his part and with it my big chance. Now naturally I want to make my name as an actor and if the star left to go into hospital it would provide me with a superb opportunity. I am a Christian and say my prayers. But what on earth am I to pray for in that situation? If the prayer of petition is being honest in the presence of God without evasion, shouldn't I be sinning against prayer if I simply asked for the star actor (let us call him George) to be kept well for the run of the play? Yet isn't that what, as a Christian, I ought to ask? I think the answer is that in the prayer of petition I have got to unload my whole heart and mind to God and tell him the whole truth. 'O God, I want to be a big success as an actor, so a large and important part of me wants George to succumb to cancer and leave. And that large and important part of me is asking precisely for that. But there is another smaller part of me, at times extremely small, which is generous and wants the best for George, and that smaller part of me is asking you to keep George fit and well. So here I am, coming into your presence with two contradictory petitions: let George's cancer develop and keep him well.' That is true prayer because it is an expression of my full self and I am not ashamed to admit that it is in a state of civil war. It is no good in

prayer pretending to myself and to God that I am
only the person who wants George to keep well.
God knows better and won't be taken in in the
slightest. God wants us to recognise honestly our
full self, and our double contradictory petition will
be a sign that we have done precisely that. When,
however, we pray 'let George's cancer develop' we
may find ourselves adding spontaneously 'Christ,
what a swine I am', and that will mean that our
prayer of petition has become a sort of confession:
an admission that a large and important part of me
needs to be healed and delivered from being a
swine. Then we will find that our true prayer has
begun to alter, begun to be less contradictory, so
that we begin to pray 'O God, make me a great
success as an actor, but without allowing any harm
to come to George. Keep him well and give me
other opportunities'. And when that happens, the
words of Jesus about Zachaeus will be true of us:
'Today has salvation come to this house'.

The point I am making is that in the prayer of
petition at all costs we must not put on our party
clothes and keep up a face saving façade. God can't
be taken in, and the only person who is taken in is
ourselves. And if we don't face our selfishness and
recognise it in our prayers it will be driven un-
derground and appear only in disguise as
something noble and good. And selfishness disguis-
ed as goodness does the maximum of harm to
everybody and especially to ourselves, like that

terrible lady who was a good woman in the worst sense of the word.

But we haven't yet touched upon the fifty thousand dollar question – does petitionary prayer work? And if so, how?

As we have seen, petitionary prayer isn't magic. That was unambiguously recognised by Jesus in Gethsemane when to the petition 'let this cup pass from me' he added 'nevertheless, not my will but thine be done'. The trouble however is that for us Christians the phrase 'if it be thy will' has become almost a meaningless formula. For example: 'when I ask Betty this evening to marry me, make her say yes, if it be thy will'. 'Help the vicar to understand me better if it be thy will.' 'Make the choir sing in tune, if it be thy will.' And the phrase as we use it is sometimes not just meaningless, because there may lurk somewhere in the background the unacknowledged suspicion that it never is God's will. Many will remember that favourite Victorian hymn 'Thy way, not mine, O Lord, however dark it be', which gives one the feeling that it is almost certainly God's will that I should fall downstairs and break my leg or something of that sort. There is no need for our renunciation of magic to turn us into pessimists.

But to repeat the question, does petition in prayer work?

You will know that there are ancient myths and legends which tell of the offer of something valuable which people will find if they seek and work for it. But after they have sought and worked for it, what they obtain is not what they imagined they would but something else, something less immediately and superficially attractive but which turns out in the end to be infinitely more valuable than the fantasy treasure that had started them off in their quest. The form of the story I remember is of an old man on his deathbed telling his three sons that there was a box of gold hidden in the field they were to inherit from him. The old man died and his sons dug and dug the field to find the gold and found nothing. But owing to their continuous digging the fruit trees in the field did marvellously well and in the end the sons came to see that it was this continuous annual crop which their father had described as the box of gold.

There is a parallel here with the prayer of petition. God knows our needs before we bring them before Him and he supplies them because it is His loving will to do so and not because of our perpetual nagging. But He knows that our greatest good, the real box of gold, is that we should trust His perfect love for us and the strength of that love to overcome all the evil and destructive forces which beset our path, including in the end, death itself. God nowhere guarantees us freedom from misfortune and suffering and certainly not from death. But He knows that the greatest good He can give us is the ability to trust Him not to let us down in the final resort but instead to fulfil His loving purpose for us – that each of us in the end should be satisfyingly, rewardingly, gloriously, without let or hindrance, his true self. That is what God did for Jesus when he raised him from the dead, and that is what God will do for us; and does do. For the resurrection to new life, although it only happens fully and completely after our physical death, begins to happen here and now. Here and now God gives us new life, new vision, new purpose, new understanding, new love, new energy. And one of the important ways in which God thus gives us new life is by our asking Him for things, because in doing that we get to know both Him better and ourselves better. And thereby we discover that the real box of gold, what we really want most, may not be what we first thought it was but something infinitely better and more satisfying. If I am ill, I still want to get well. If I am in danger of losing my job, I still don't want to lose it. If I am an actor I still want to be a star. But in telling God honestly and trustfully about these things I get to know Him and love Him more, which means I realise more fully how His love enfolds me everywhere and will never let me go, even when I die. To realise in this way God's utterly faithful love to me is infinitely better than becoming a star actor, or even not losing my job or not recovering from an illness. But of course, God may and most likely will reveal His love to me by making me well or enabling me to keep the job or become a star actor. For the

love of God don't let us start with the prejudice that
God doesn't want any of the nice things to happen.
God often creates us by health and security and
success. But what He wants most is for us to find
our true selves in His love. And we find our true
selves very largely by the natural child-like trust-
fulness of the prayer of petition. So don't let us be
taken in by the spiritual snobs. Prayer does mean
asking for things.

5. Prayer as Intercession

This chapter is about intercession, that is, praying for other people.

We need the same honesty and naturalness in praying for others as in praying for ourselves. For instance, in a week or two, thousands of children in Britain will be taking exams, O and A levels. But it is no good my pretending that I am concerned about all of them. My real concern is for my son Johnny who is taking his A-levels and my daughter Betty who is taking her O-levels. So it is for them that I shall pray, and quite rightly, because it is Johnny and Betty that God has given me to be specially concerned about.

Praying for others depends upon their being real for me, and those closest to me are naturally the most real. But other people can become real to me by the use of my imagination. When my imagination is stirred people I have never met or only heard of or read about can become very real to me. And thus I can become sincerely concerned about them and their affairs and therefore pray for them. That is where great novelists and dramatists and poets can be of enormous use in our prayer. They open the eyes of our imagination to see what is really going on behind people's exterior façade. We begin through the eyes of a novelist or dramatist or poet to appreciate the dreams, struggles, joys, sufferings, conflicts, victories which are the inner reality of that apparently rather boringly ordinary woman Mrs. Smith, or that apparently irritatingly conceited man Mr. Jones. What our imagination can do for individuals, it can also sometimes do for whole peoples and cultures. When for instance Solzhenitsyn puts before us in horrifyingly concrete detail what it is like to live under the brutal tyranny of a police state, then the plight of those who do is sharply brought home to us and we are deeply concerned about them and pray for them. In a previous chapter, I said that study, reading about Christian doctrine etc. is for people like us an essential preliminary to prayer as being in God's presence. The same sort of thing is true of the prayer of intercession. Because it depends upon our imagination, our imagination needs to be fed. And it needs to be fed even, or perhaps especially, with regard to the people who are closest to us – wives, husbands, children, and so on. Our imagination needs to bring home to us what is really going on inside them and how they are changing, because to live is to change. We may need dramatists and poets to open our eyes to what is really happening at our own dining room table. But with regard to people less close to us we need to be fed with information. If for instance, we feel called to pray for the peoples of Russia or Southern Africa, then we must take steps to be reasonably well informed about them. Or if we feel called to pray for Mary who is having a nervous breakdown or for Richard and Susan whose marriage looks like breaking up, then our prayers demand that we should keep ourselves reasonably up to date with the state of affairs. The trouble this involves is part of the prayer of intercession. I don't personally think that it is much good having what I would call fossils in our prayer list – people with whom we have been out of contact for a very long time and who don't look as if they will ever cross our path again. This seems to me to be an obvious practical measure because the limited time at our disposal means that we can pray only for a certain amount of particular individuals, and as the present needs of new people are brought to our notice we may well have to strike out those with whom we have lost contact or whose crisis seems to have been resolved. There is no reason to feel guilty about this. It is a matter of obvious common sense. In my experience we need fairly constantly to revise our prayer lists, though of course some people, those we love, will be on it for life. And by that I mean our life not theirs, since of course we can continue to pray for them after they have passed beyond this present world.

I make no apologies for the humdrum nature of what I have said, because prayer depends very much on practical matters like those just mentioned. If prayer is no more than being swept away on a cloud of emotion which we can mistake for spirituality, then it won't get very far or last very long. Perhaps in the matter of prayer we take too little notice of the parable of the unjust steward. Dishonest rogue though he was, he did some hard thinking about the situation he was in and took some extremely practical steps. It was for being practical that he was commended.

But now we must make for the centre of what we are considering. It can be summed up in two interrelated questions. What is the prayer of intercession? And how are we to pray for others? Like the prayer of petition, intercession isn't magic nor is it wringing concessions for others out of a reluctant Deity. We wouldn't think of it consciously quite in those terms, but it is sometimes in the background of our minds – push God two or three times more and, who knows? He may do it. I think perhaps the parable of the importunate widow has been misunderstood here. The parable teaches us that persistence in prayer pays. It doesn't teach us that God is like the discreditable judge who disregarded the rights and wrongs of of the widow's plea and gave her what she wanted because he found her continuous nagging intolerable. As you will remember in the Sermon on the Mount Jesus warned us against the mistake of imagining that we shall be heard for our much speaking.

Another mistake we sometimes fall into is to think of intercession as instructing God precisely what to do for somebody. Many years ago when I was a very young priest a wife wrote to me, asking me to pray for her husband. She wrote: 'He needs promotion in his job to increase his confidence and earn a little more money, but it must be a small promotion and a small increase of salary. So don't pray that he gets a job near the top. That would go to his head. Pray that he just gets up one step on the ladder. Also on leaving the office after work he needs a drink with friends in the pub, so pray that he may continue to do this, but also pray that he won't spend more than say twenty to twenty-five minutes in the pub, so that he can catch the 6.33 train home from Victoria, not the 7.05.' Well, poor man, I guess he certainly needed praying for. Now of course, that is an extreme instance of telling God what to do and I realise that when we are very concerned about somebody it is often difficult to strike the right balance in intercession. Naturally we want our children Johnny and Betty to pass their exams and it is stupid and unnatural to try to disguise this fact when we pray for them. But we have to keep things in proportion and realise that their passing may not be in the long run the best thing for them, however desirable it looks at the present.

The real basis of intercession is the fact which, in traditional christian language, is called the communion of saints. We are not isolated entities, each person locked up in himself and impenetrable, individual islands surrounded by seas which nobody can pass over. On the contrary, in the inside of life, in the invisible world, we are all of us, the whole of mankind, closely and deeply interrelated. Our outward contact with each other by sight and hearing and touch is no more than the tip of an iceberg. Outward contact is no more than the visible sign of a far more real, deeper, and closer contact we all have with each other in the most real world there is. St. Paul expounded this truth in his teaching about the Body of Christ, and the Body of Christ is potentially mankind as a whole. He says: 'If one member suffers, all suffer together, if one member is honoured, all rejoice together'. In deepest truth we all belong to one another, we all cohere in each other. That is why I must love my neighbour as myself, because in an important sense my neighbour is myself. And my neighbour, as Jesus showed us in the parable of the Good Samaritan, is anybody in need.

Because of the communion of saints, the mystery of the Body of Christ, because we are all very closely interrelated, therefore none of us can enter into the presence of God simply for himself alone. However and whenever we pray and whatever the form of our prayers, our communion with God always flows out from us to mankind. But since mankind as a whole is far too large a concept for our limited imagination, we can't pray with much meaning for all men everywhere. We have to particularise, praying for particular people or peoples, those we love or those in need, individuals whose plight had been brought home to us or collectivities like the peoples of Russia or Southern Africa. We lift up our hearts to the Lord so that we may become aware of His presence with us and then in God's presence we think of the person we are praying for. Sometimes we shall do no more than present him to the Lord, cover him, if you like, with God's presence in a general sort or way. And sometimes we shall feel led to mention some overriding need he has at the moment: he is ill, or depressed or is finding his job difficult or his wife has recently died. We shall just think of his need and not tell God what to do about it. Sometimes he won't be in any particular need, and we may find ourselves just talking to God about him, especially the people we love and pray for always. We talk about his family and children, his work, his strength and weaknesses, his happiness and worries, presenting him to the Lord sometimes in fairly quick detail. And don't let us forget St. Paul's word 'by prayer and supplication with thanksgiving', teaching us to give thanks for all men. Part of intercession is giving thanks for people, and sometimes our intercession for a person will take the form of giving thanks for him and nothing more. 'Thank you God for creating such a wonderful person as Betty or John.'

In intercession we pray for the sake of others, not

for ourselves. But our intercession inevitably rebounds on us. It rebounds in two chief ways which are mysteriously intertwined – in pain and in joy.

When we present somebody's need or pain to God we must be prepared in some way or other, in some degree or other, to share the pain. I don't mean that we should try to make ourselves artificially miserable, because that would be sheer self-indulgence – few things are so enjoyable as being miserable. Nor do I mean that there will be any literal identity between my pain and the pain of the person I am praying for. There can't be, since our temperaments and circumstances are different. He has got cancer and I haven't. But in the lives of us all there will come uninvited from time to time things which are difficult, disturbing, painful, even sometimes agonising. And intercession teaches us that these things are not just for ourselves alone. We can do more with them than grin hard and bear them, though we may have to do that as well. Though probably in a completely different form they can be seen as our share of the pain afflicting the people we are praying for, so that our own difficulty or misfortune or pain or whatever it is can be recognised as a most important part of our prayer for others. Let us say I am in perplexity or distress, some sort of pain, physical or mental. It means that I have at least some small thing in common (perhaps it won't be so small) with John who

72

has just lost his wife or with the persecuted Christians in Russia. And that something in common, my distress of whatever kind, I can use as my prayer for John or for persecuted Christians or whatever it may be. Put it like this: in some small way I have been allowed to share Christ's cross and so has John or those being persecuted. And my realisation of our togetherness on Christ's cross is intercession perhaps at its highest. Jesus on the cross offered Himself to God for mankind. Intercession means sharing in that offering of Jesus on the cross for mankind. But with us, because of our limited imagination, mankind has to be represented by particular people or peoples. We can't pray for people unless we are at least prepared to find ourselves in some way or other with them and with Jesus on the cross. So if and when our life really becomes a mess and we find ourselves one wide wound all of us, then let us open our eyes to see the marvellous and sacred privilege which is being granted to us, the privilege of sharing with Jesus in the cost of healing and restoring mankind. It is easy to be selfish about our sufferings. But if we are, they remain no more than a dead end, when they could be the very centre and mainspring of our prayer for others.

But with the pain there is intertwined joy. Sometimes the joy in intercession is straightforward, because in our prayers we remember people who are happy and full of zest for life and we realise our oneness with them in the Lord. Something of their happiness and zest bounces back on us. We give thanks for them because what they have is really ours too. But more often the joy of intercession is the joy of Christ raised from the dead because He was crucified. It is in the light of the resurrection that we see the cross on which those we pray for are nailed. In sharing the cross with them we also share the resurrection. It means the joy of knowing that nothing in heaven or on earth, nothing in life or in death, can separate us from the love of God. It is the joy of abundant and indestructible life springing out of death itself, and so out of misfortune and suffering.

Part of our own and most other people's pain is their sense of isolation, their sense of being in the last resort alone. 'I, a stranger and afraid in a world I never made.' In intercession we begin to realise that we are not alone, that in fact we are in living and active communion with all people living and departed. But since, once again, that is too big a concept for our imagination, we know ourselves to be in living and active communion with the people we love or who have impinged upon us in some way or other.

I can't speak truthfully without some sacrifice of reticence. So, may I say this? – people sometimes ask me (though it is eight years ago since I left): 'After Cambridge don't you feel rather isolated in Mirfield? ' Well, the answer is that I don't, quite the reverse. I am very much luckier than most of you since, in spite of the chores I described earlier, our timetable at Mirfield does allow us regular periods for intercession. And because of this I am much closer to everybody I love and am interested in than I ever was before. More accurately, I am able through intercession to realise how close to them I am, even if they are hundreds of miles away or I see them very rarely, realise it more than I ever did before. I have discovered that part of the joy of intercession is the joy of fellowship, of real fundamental contact with people, of knowing that we are all one in the Lord.

I am going to give just a final postscript. If our prayer for others becomes an excuse not to act on their behalf, not to do what we can for them, then of course we can be certain that our prayer is bogus. Real prayer leads to action, leads to our doing what we can for people. But it also saves us from fantasies of omnipotence, of imagining that we can do for people what we manifestly can't do, and from the anxiety and guilt-feelings such fantasies evoke. And praying for people also makes us sensitive to their deepest needs which are generally not their most obvious ones. By means of our prayer God succours people in the very centre and core of their being, and that is what they need most.

6. Conclusion – Prayer as One

So far I have discussed the various kinds of prayer such as meditation, petition, intercession, and how our understanding or misunderstanding of them can help or hinder us. I have kept the discussion on that elementary level because that is the level to which I myself belong and it would be stupid of me to talk of things of which I have no experience. Yet even so I realise that there has been a certain degree of unreality or artificiality in what I have said. But that is bound to happen when something which is a living whole is chopped up into bits for the purposes of analysis and description. The various kinds of prayer I have attempted to describe are not really distinct from one another. In fact they all coalesce into one single loving response to God's love for us. All prayer is one living whole. And it is prayer as a living whole that I shall discuss in this final chapter.

Prayer is communion with God like that between two friends who know each other intimately. In the Bible people are described as the friends of God. The Lord, we are told, used to speak to Moses face to face as a man speaks to his friend, while the Epistle of St. James says of Abraham that he was called the friend of God. And there is no need for us to be reminded of our Lord in St. John's gospel calling His disciples His friends. But prayer is not only that. It is also awe and wonder and praise. Such awe, wonder, and praise is something we can be caught up in as we join in communal worship in church. But it may sound a bit unreal to describe awe, wonder, and praise as a church service because, as we all know, a church service can often be dull if not depressing. Let us therefore describe the prayer which is awe and wonder and praise as parallel to what we feel when we are confronted with something of superlative grandeur and beauty – a landscape, the ocean rolling in fullest pride, the magnificence of some blazing thunderstorm, the deep tranquillity of a remote countryside, a work of art which fascinates and compels. Such things indeed not only illustrate the wonder, awe, and praise we feel in God's presence. They are true and valid instances of it. For God's transcendence, what in picture language we describe as His being infinitely above and beyond us, is mediated to us by His immanence, by His being there in His transcendent majesty, in the landscape, the ocean, the thunderstorm, the countryside, the picture by Turner or the symphony by Mozart. That is what we mean when we say that we live in a sacramental universe. The world is charged with the grandeur of God. It will flame out.

But not only in what we call majestic and

beautiful things. (Prayer in those circumstances is often easy enough.) But at the very heart of Christian prayer and adoration there is the glory of God revealed in the foul darkness of Calvary. And so prayer is also the vision of God in all that is perverted, ugly, cruel, sick, horrible, death-dealing. Prayer is fully facing the loathsome reality of all these evil things and seeing within them the greater reality, the ultimate reality, of God's glory; the transforming, converting, lifegiving power of His love, even in the corpse of a murdered man. Prayer is seeing Calvary, wherever it may be or whatever form it may take, in the light of Easter and its triumphant joy.

Some years ago I was travelling in a third-class carriage from Paris to Chartres and with me in the compartment were a peasant and his daughter of round about 20. The girl suddenly had a frightful epileptic fit, screaming and convulsing and frothing at the mouth. I was aware only of the horror of it. It was the girl's father who opened my eyes by the tenderness and love and support he gave to his daughter. He was totally concerned for her, compassionate in a completely practical way, without the slightest hint of being a ministering angel or of any other sort of condescension. That was the form his prayer took in those circumstances, and it revealed evil swallowed up by goodness. I realised that I had seen something which not even all the stained glass at Chartres could show me. Our railway compartment had become the house of God and the gate of heaven.

Anybody would have seen that. It was easy. What is difficult is to see the gate of heaven when there appears to be nothing but sickness and evil, without any visible good swallowing it up. Yet that is precisely what prayer often is, seeing Him who is invisible, the Saviour, and worshipping Him in His glory when the glory is revealed in His sacred head sore wounded, defiled and put to scorn. And the wounds won't all belong to other people. Many of them will be our own wounds, the subtle psychic wounds which lurk in our own depths and which we are often too frightened to look at or even to admit to ourselves, those elements of us which are unlovely because in some way or other in our early days we were unloved and our intrinsic tenderness was violated. Prayer is the recognition of those wounds as the gate of heaven, the places where above all God is incarnate now in us. So that seeing God's healing presence with us in our wounds we bow down before Him in wonder and praise and sing in our hearts of His love to the loveless shown that they might lovely be.

There is a superb image of what I am trying to say in Dostoyevsky's *Crime and Punishment*. Marmeladov, a wastrel who has allowed his daughter Sonia to become a prostitute in order to provide the wherewithal to feed his family, is drunk as usual in a tavern and imagines to the publican all the drunkards being summoned before the judge-ment seat. Marmeladov says: 'And we shall all come forth without shame and shall stand before him, and he will say to us: "you are swine, made in the image of the beast and bearing his mark. But come to me, you also." And the wise men will say: "Lord, why does thou receive these men?" And he will say: "this is why I receive them, oh wise men, because not one of them believed himself to be worthy of this". And he will hold out his hands to us and we shall fall down before him and we shall weep and we shall understand all things.' We shall understand all things. In prayer we enter into the realm of reality and see things as they really are, from God's point of view.

One of the obstacles to our understanding this is that often we imagine that something is either real or unreal, when in fact there are degrees of reality and unreality, differing shades of grey as well as black and white. And we can pass, so to speak, from the most real to what is still real but less real through the least real to the unreal. And this pass-ing through degrees of reality is further complicated in the Christian scheme by the fact that it is worked out in terms of time as an order of succession, one thing happening after another. So, on Good Friday, Jesus was crucified, and there you had evil, evil as reality. But on the third day after He rose from the dead, and in the light of His resurrection the real evil of Good Friday was seen to be transformed by something infinitely more real, God's lifegiving love which transformed the worst day in history into the best, so that we call that Friday Good.

Prayer is not escapism. It is not a running away from the brute ugly facts of a situation into an illusory never-never land. Prayer is an acceptance of the reality of evil and suffering and death, while at the same time seeing these penultimate realities in the light of the ultimate and final and most real reality of God's love, victorious over everything which opposes it. And so in prayer we see things as they really are, finally and ultimately from God's point of view, the God for whom past, present, and future are all one. That is what enabled Julian of Norwich to say 'All shall be well and all manner of things shall be well'. It wasn't a cranky optimism. It was an apprehension that Christ is risen and God reigns. It was similar apprehension which led Henry Vaughan to say 'Prayer is the world in tune'. When we pray we pass from partial insights, which may be true as far as they go, and live in the context of the whole. That is why people of prayer invariably have a profound sense of humour which makes them such good company. They are people who care; they care more than anybody else. But at the same time they also realise that in the end nothing matters because Christ is risen and God reigns. And so they can laugh at the extraordinary and bizarre contrast between reality as it looks from an earthbound point of view and the same reality as it looks from the pont of view of God's ultimate victory. But of course they don't work it out each time in terms of those dry theological concepts. They feel the contrast immediately by their spiritual intuition and laugh at once spontaneously.

There is for instance a very well-known story, about St Teresa of Avila. When by a misadventure on a journey all the luggage fell into a river, she didn't say to her nuns, we will now sing the doxology! As we know, she said to our Lord, 'No wonder you have so few friends if you treat them so badly'. There you have humour and love deliciously combined.

I remember a cartoon I saw in *The Tatler* round about 1950, which showed two girls emerging into the street from a nightclub. One of them said: 'What a funny smell'. To which her friend answered: 'Yes, can it be the fresh air?'. It is the fresh air we breathe when we pray, God's fresh air, and it puts everything into its right context, so that we see our lives and the world in a true perspective. And it often means that instead of desperately hankering after things, we see that they are not anything like so important as we thought. Indeed, they may be revealed as just emptiness and vanity, though not necessarily so. I mean things like personal prestige or worldly success or even having a wife and family to love and care about. We shall laugh at the contrast between ourselves, our feelings and desires, when we are at prayer, and ourselves when we have returned again to the real, but less real, world. Like my favourite Edwardian lady who, getting into her carriage after a reception, said to her friend: 'Eternity rings in my ears but little things matter so much'. And maybe the things will not be so little.

For anybody who talks about prayer there is a besetting temptation. It consists of presenting prayer as a universal tranquilliser, a sort of spritual librium, like the fat millionaire in Aldous Huxley's *After Many a Summer* who every time he felt at all disturbed by anything used to say 'God is love, there is no death'.

It is true, as St Paul said, that 'the fruits of the spirit are love, joy, peace'. But that statement has to be understood deeply not superficially. We are all of us in some degree or other alienated from our truest selves. My truest self is the place within me where God dwells. And in prayer I begin to have access to my truest self, for prayer as well as being a lifting-up of my heart and mind to God on high is also at the same time a going-down deep into myself and finding God there.

But, in order to arrive at my truest self where God dwells, it is necessary for me to pass through some pretty rough and decidedly ugly country. To find God within me I have on the way to encounter aspects of myself from which I tend to run away and hide. For instance, there is the would-be omnipotent infant, the wounded and therefore savage child, the wretched depressed person feeling totally dependent upon other people's good opinion of him, or the one who feels utterly powerless and can't face it and therefore plays hide and seek with himself. 'I may be powerless but look at my brains, my business success, my important friends, my exciting sex life, my car and my clothes.' I have not only to encounter all those ugly aspects of myself, I have also to learn to accept and receive them as valid aspects of what I am. Indeed I have to learn to love them as I would love a naughty and wayward child. And that can't be done without considerable turmoil. So my prayer, my search for the presence and peace of God within me, will compel me to pass through ugliness and perhaps agony. I shall find God within me all right. I shall find the love and joy and peace which is my truest self. But the discovery will for a long time be mixed up with the pain and discomforts of the journey. What in due time will happen is that slowly (though not gradually but by fits and starts) I shall become more aware of God's presence within and less aware of the turmoil of the journey because, having found my truest self as God's presence within me, I shall be able to accept and receive the more superficial aspects of myself with less difficulty and pain. And the more I am thus able to accept and receive the more superficial aspects of myself, the less important will they be and the less harm will they do. They will begin to diminish and even disappear. In the end (which extremely few people reach here on earth, only the saints) I shall be so aware of God's presence within me that the rest of me will be totally transfigured by it. And then I shall really know how perfect love, God's love, casts out fear.

But even so, the result will hardly be like that of a tranquilliser. Perfect love may cast out fear, but perfect love is also totally vulnerable as we see in the person of the Crucified. Lovelessness is an attempt at invulnerability. So we should be glad if we are vulnerable. It means that we can love and are finding our truest selves where God is.

A further consequence of finding my truest self as God in me is that it may at least for a time take away from me all sense of God as other. I may for the time being have to find God in what I am or not at all. And this may mean that religion in the more usual sense may, at least temporarily, pack up on me altogether. The hymns and prayers and services and liturgies which once meant a great deal to me may become meaningless and my private prayer may cease to have the warm intimacy of communion with God and land me in darkness. But it will be the dazzling darkness described by St. John of the Cross which in its very darkness is apprehended as compelling in its absolute value, the one pearl of great price for which I am willing to sell all my warm cosy feelings. That may happen or it may not. The thing is to be prepared for it to happen in case it does. And if it does, we shall find ourselves saying with Mary Magdalen 'They have taken away my Lord and I know not where they have laid him', so that to us as to her the living Lord may be revealed, the Lord who says '*Noli me tangere*; do not cling to me', for He must be within me as my truest self and not beside me like a friend.

A Sufi man of prayer who lived in the late fifteenth century, an Indian called Kabir, said: 'If thy soul' (by which he mean my truest self) 'if thy soul is a stranger to thee the whole world becomes unhomely'. Kabir here is talking of prayerlessness. Let us consider the opposite: prayerfulness. When we are people of prayer and discover God's presence within us as our truest self then we perceive even our enemies as our friends. And by enemies I don't only mean other people, but the enemies of temperament and circumstance. When we are people of prayer we discover that all things are ours, the world or life or death or the present or the future. We discover that all are ours, and we are Christ's and Christ is God's. So, no wonder, people of prayer are people of power: the power to love, to suffer, to laugh, to enjoy; the power to be: to be fully what they most truly are.